FLORID
VICTORIAN
ORNAMENT

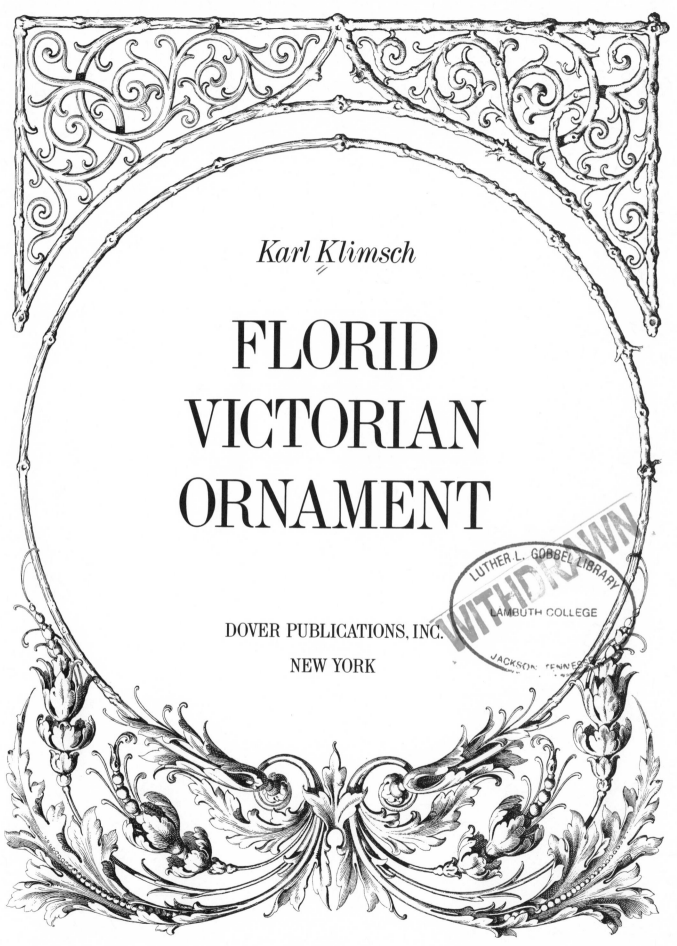

Karl Klimsch

FLORID VICTORIAN ORNAMENT

DOVER PUBLICATIONS, INC.

NEW YORK

Published in Canada by General Publishing
Company, Ltd., 30 Lesmill Road, Don Mills,
Toronto, Ontario.
Published in the United Kingdom by Constable
and Company, Ltd., 10 Orange Street, London
WC2H 7EG.

Florid Victorian Ornament, first published by
Dover Publications, Inc., in 1977, is an unabridged
republication of the work *Ornaments Invented
& Designed by Charles Klimsch* as published by
London, Asher & Co. in London, n.d. (title and
imprint in English, the plates all inscribed "Kunst-
Verlag von Karl Klimsch, Frankfurt a/Main" or
close variants).

DOVER *Pictorial Archive* SERIES

International Standard Book Number: 0-486-23490-8
Library of Congress Catalog Card Number: 76-58573

Manufactured in the United States of America
Dover Publications, Inc.
31 East 2nd Street
Mineola, N.Y. 11501

Ornaments

INVENTED & DESIGNED
BY
CHARLES KLIMSCH

Original title-page design.

PLATE 1

PLATE 2

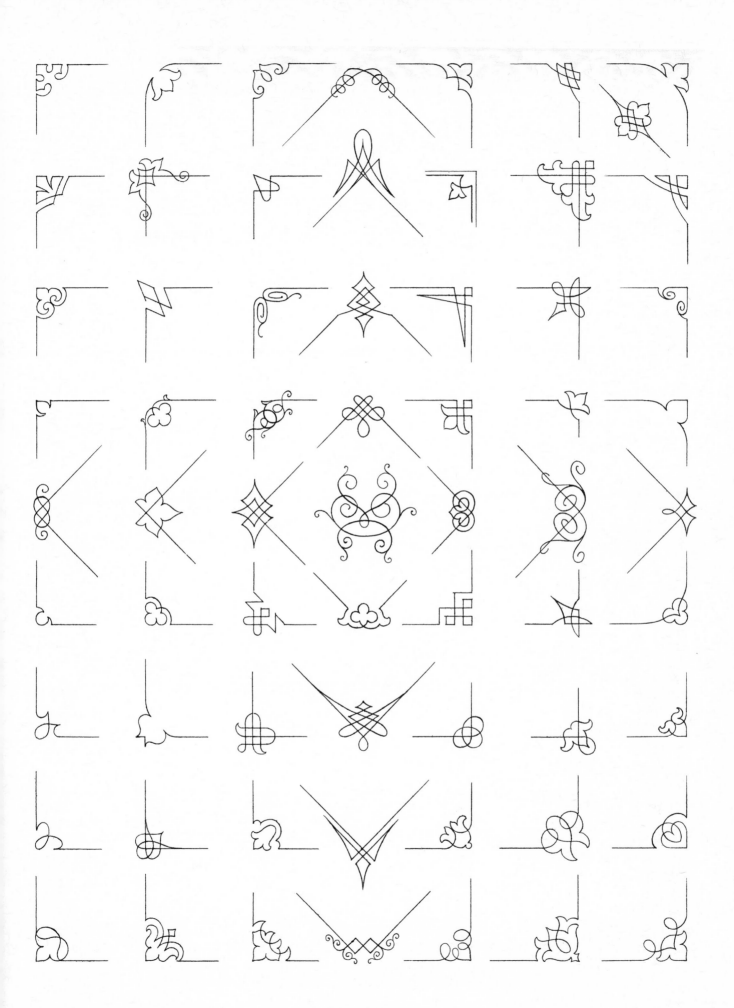

PLATE 3

PLATE 4

PLATE 5

PLATE 6

PLATE 7

PLATE 8

PLATE 9

PLATE 10

PLATE 11

PLATE 12

PLATE 13

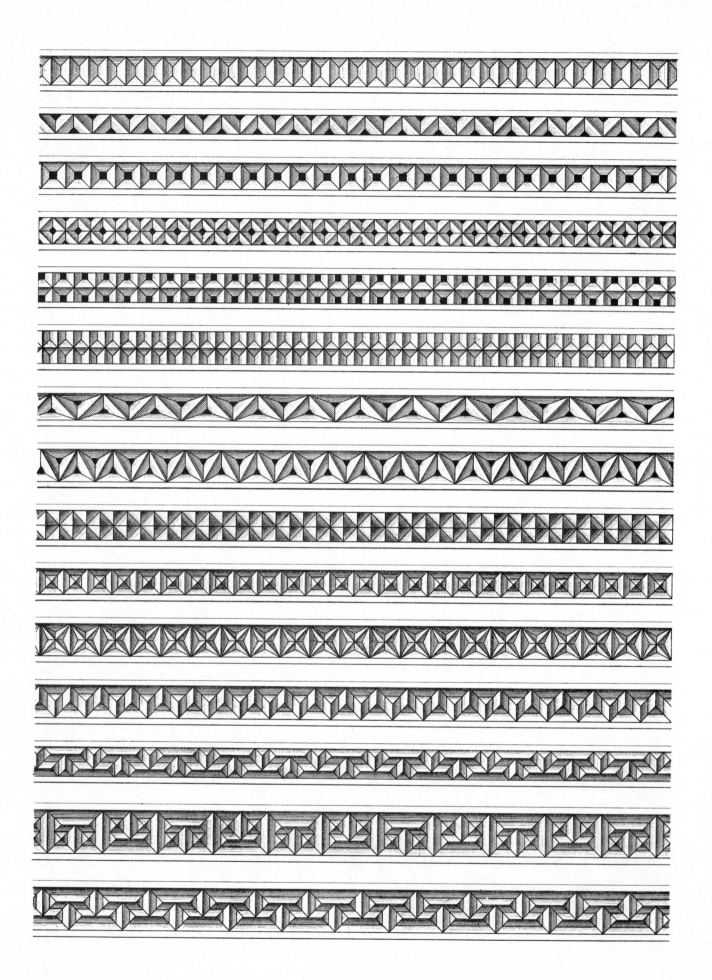

PLATE 14

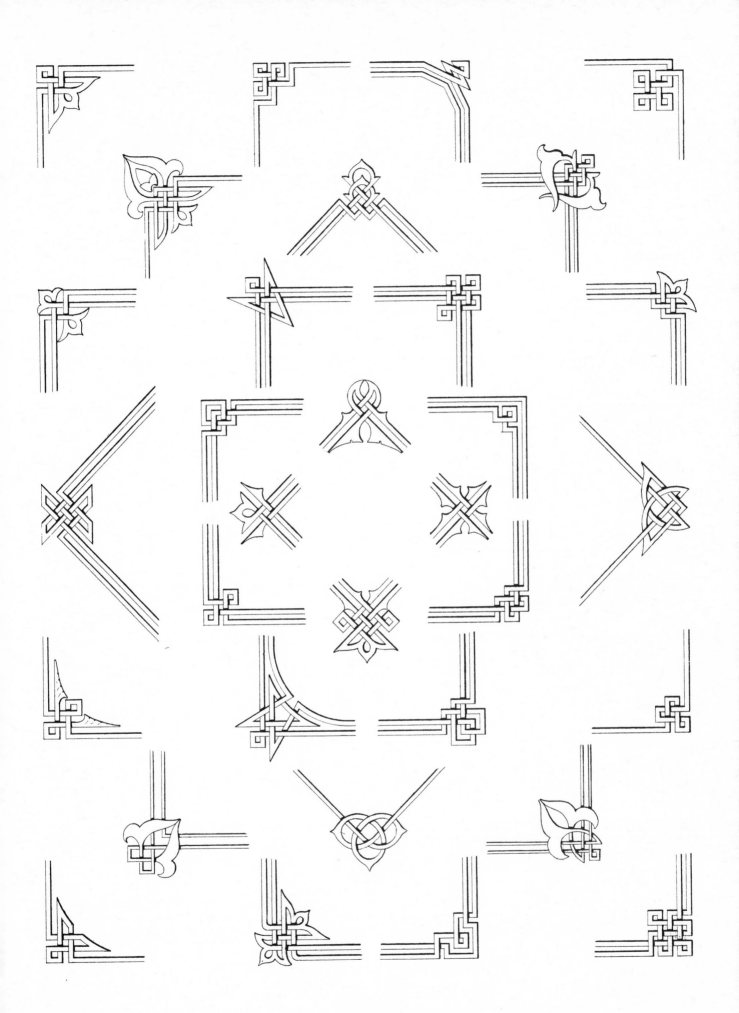

PLATE 15

PLATE 16

PLATE 17

PLATE 18

PLATE 19

PLATE 20

PLATE 21

PLATE 22

PLATE 23

PLATE 24

PLATE 25

PLATE 26

PLATE 27

PLATE 28

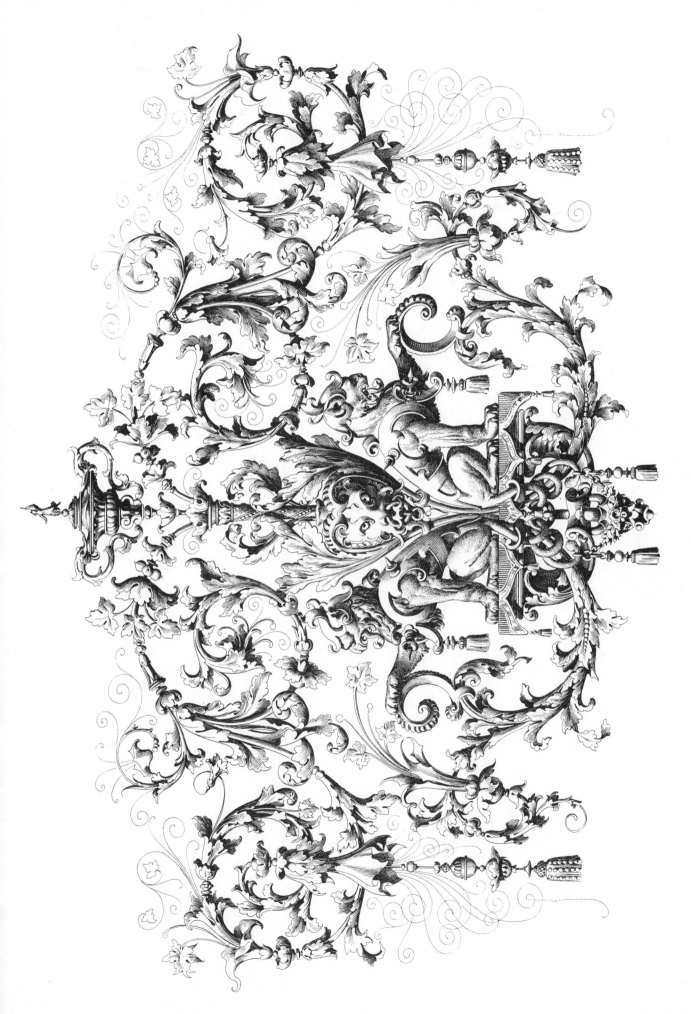

PLATE 29

PLATE 30

PLATE 31

PLATE 32

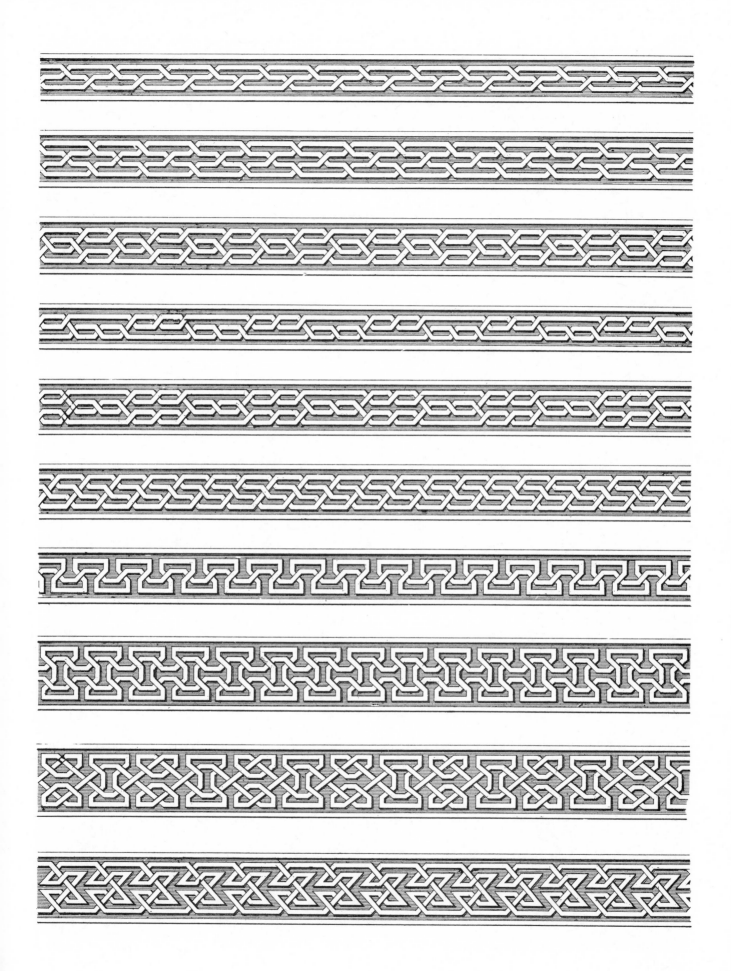

PLATE 33

PLATE 34

PLATE 35

PLATE 36

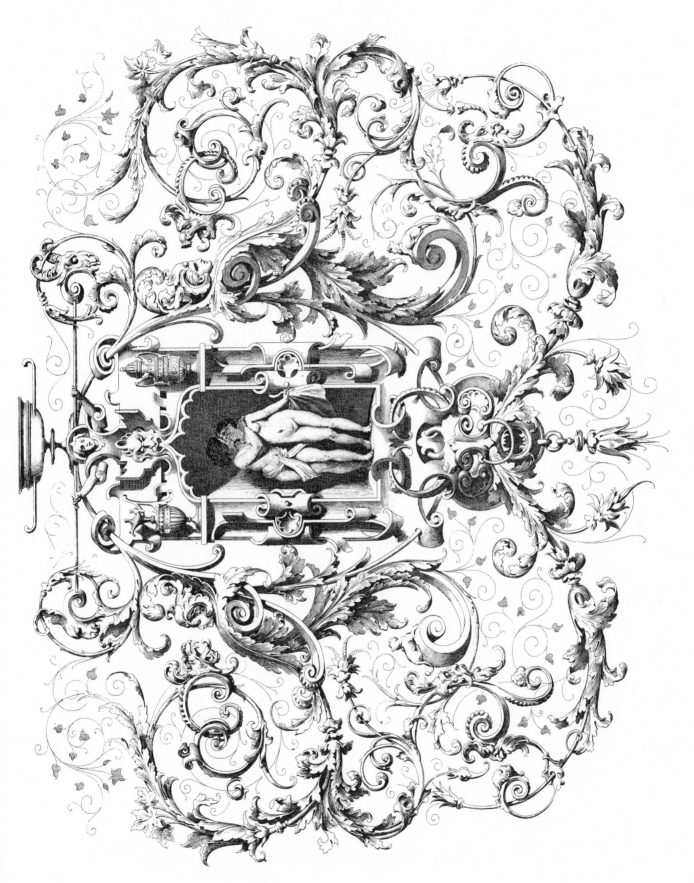

PLATE 37

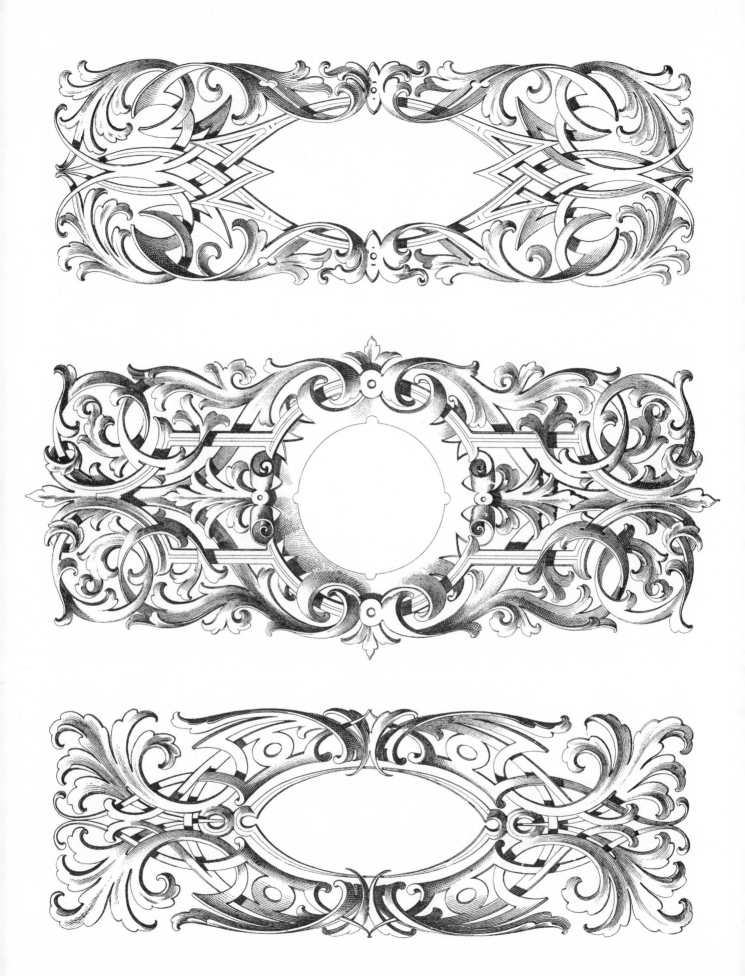

PLATE 38

PLATE 39

PLATE 40

PLATE 41

PLATE 42

PLATE 43

PLATE 44

PLATE 45

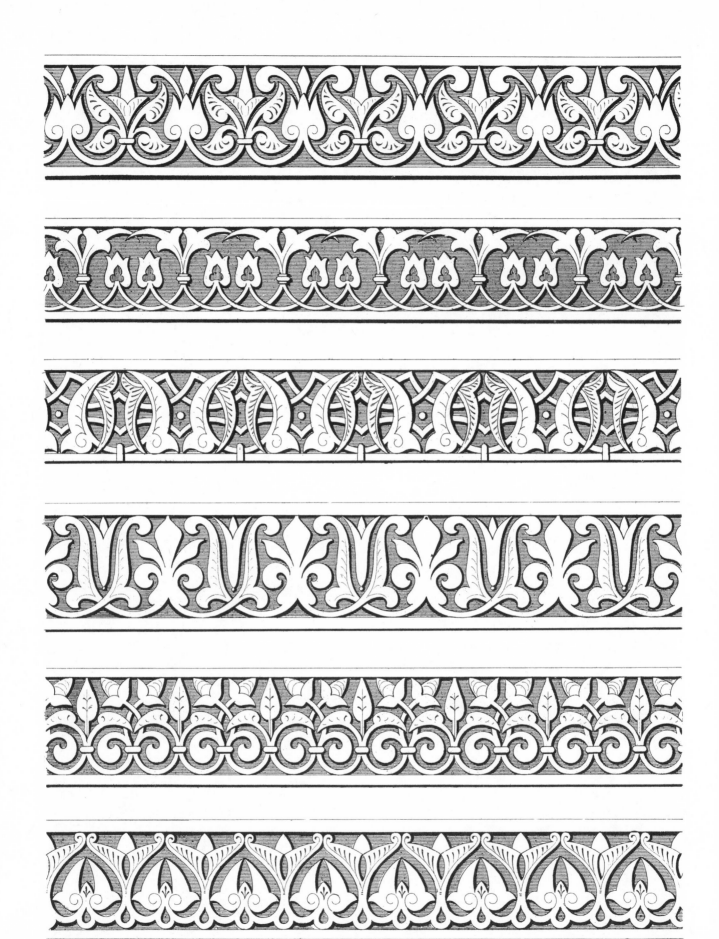

PLATE 46

PLATE 47

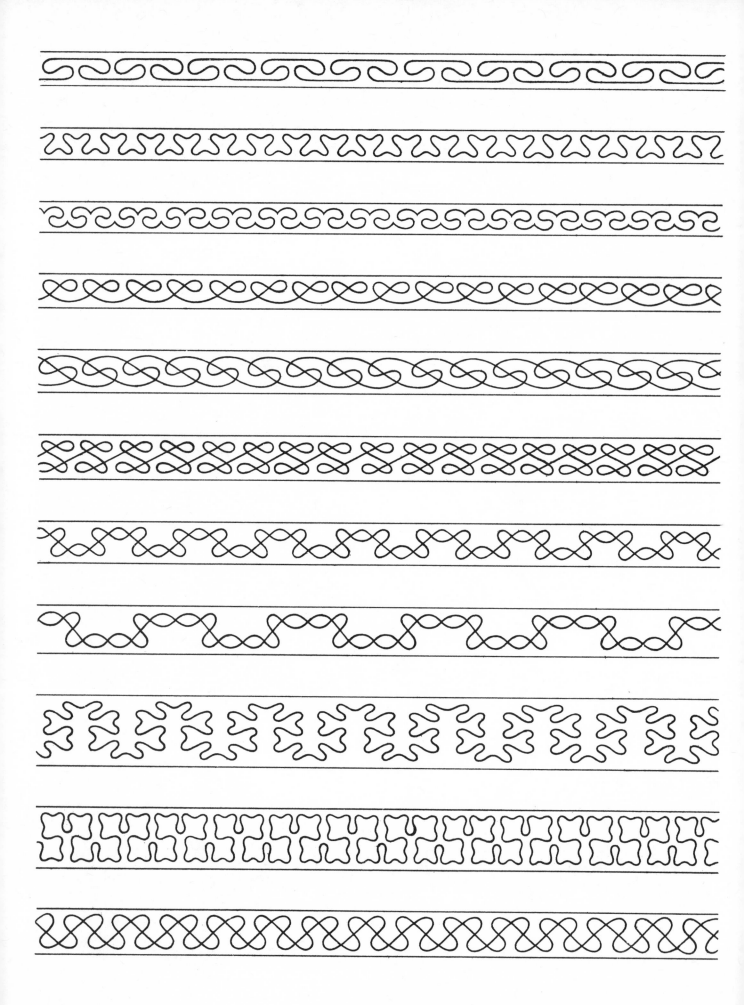

PLATE 48

PLATE 49

PLATE 50

PLATE 51

PLATE 52

PLATE 53

PLATE 54

PLATE 55

PLATE 56

PLATE 57

PLATE 58

PLATE 59

PLATE 60

PLATE 61

PLATE 62

PLATE 63

PLATE 64

PLATE 65

PLATE 66

PLATE 67

PLATE 68

PLATE 69

PLATE 70

PLATE 71

PLATE 72

PLATE 73

PLATE 74

PLATE 75

PLATE 76

PLATE 77

PLATE 78

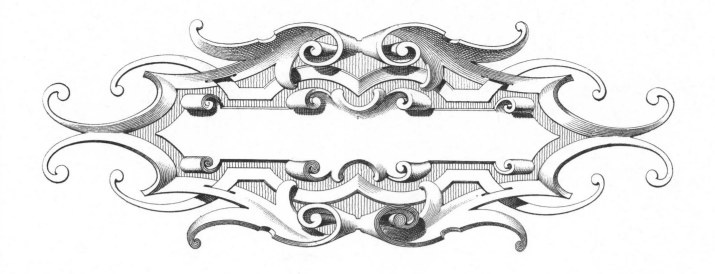

PLATE 79

PLATE 80

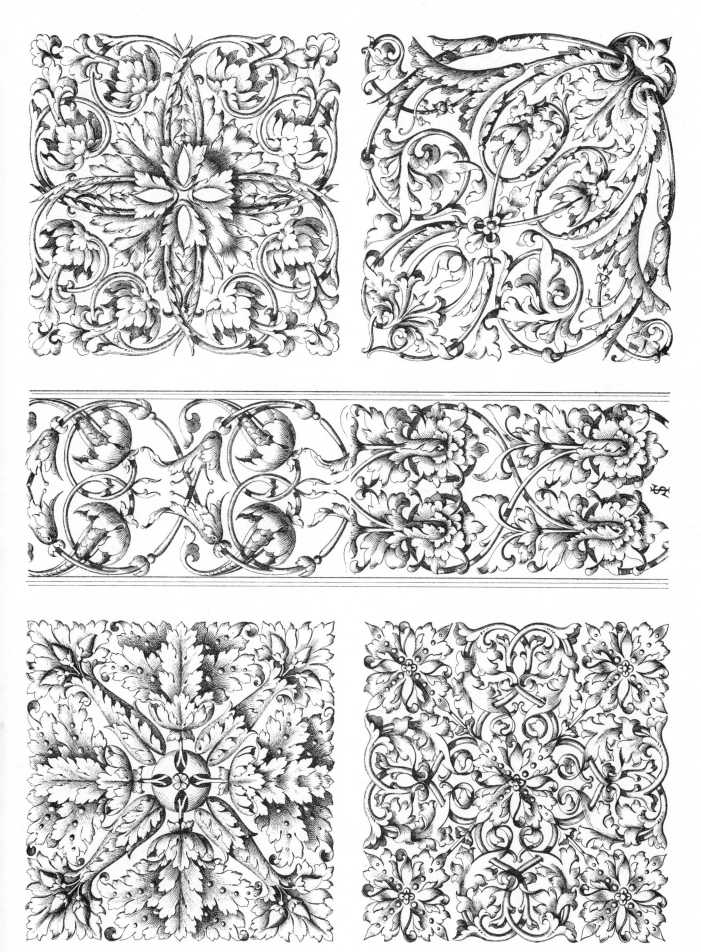

PLATE 81

PLATE 82

PLATE 83

PLATE 84

PLATE 85

PLATE 86

PLATE 87

PLATE 88

BURLESQUE

PLATE 89

PLATE 90

PLATE 91

PLATE 92

PLATE 93

PLATE 94

PLATE 95

PLATE 96

PLATE 97

PLATE 98

PLATE 99

PLATE 100

PLATE 101

PLATE 102